THE POETRY OF THULIUM

The Poetry of Thulium

Walter the Educator

Silent King Books a WhichHead Imprint

Copyright © 2024 by Walter the Educator

All rights reserved. No part of this book may be reproduced in any manner whatsoever without written permission except in the case of brief quotations embodied in critical articles and reviews.

First Printing, 2024

Disclaimer
This book is a literary work; poems are not about specific persons, locations, situations, and/or circumstances unless mentioned in a historical context. This book is for entertainment and informational purposes only. The author and publisher offer this information without warranties expressed or implied. No matter the grounds, neither the author nor the publisher will be accountable for any losses, injuries, or other damages caused by the reader's use of this book. The use of this book acknowledges an understanding and acceptance of this disclaimer.

"Earning a degree in chemistry changed my life!"
- Walter the Educator

dedicated to all the chemistry lovers, like myself, across the world

CONTENTS

Dedication v

Why I Created This Book? 1

One - Oh Thulium 2

Two - Magnificent Creation 4

Three - Symbol Of Grace 6

Four - Boundless Love 8

Five - Presence Echoes 10

Six - Glimpse The Unknown 12

Seven - Thulium Divine 14

Eight - Shining In The Dark 16

Nine - Limitless World 18

Ten - Human Curiosity 19

Eleven - To Thulium 20

Twelve - Surreal 22

Thirteen - Lifelong Dream	. . . . .	23
Fourteen - Inspire	. . . .	24
Fifteen - Scientific Anthem	. . . .	26
Sixteen - Discovery's Quest	. . . .	28
Seventeen - Shimmer And Gleam	. . . . . .	30
Eighteen - Atomic Embrace	. . . .	32
Nineteen - Power Shines	. . . .	34
Twenty - Lasers To Alloys	. . . .	35
Twenty-One - The Best	. . . .	36
Twenty-Two - Advancing Technology	. . . .	37
Twenty-Three - Oh Thulium, Conductor	. . . .	39
Twenty-Four - Within The Deep	. . . .	41
Twenty-Five - Intricate Design	. . . .	43
Twenty-Six - Elemental Chase	. . . .	44
Twenty-Seven - Phenomenon To Behold	. . .	46
Twenty-Eight - Silent Hero	. . . .	48
Twenty-Nine - Pure And Light	. . . .	49
Thirty - Radiant Voice	. . . .	50
Thirty-One - Dance Of Photons	. . . .	52
Thirty-Two - Day By Day	. . . .	54

Thirty-Three - Admiration 56

Thirty-Four - Infinite Worth 58

About The Author 60

WHY I CREATED THIS BOOK?

Creating a poetry book about the chemical element Thulium is a unique and creative way to explore science, blend art with academia, and engage readers in a distinctive manner.

ONE

OH THULIUM

In the depths of the periodic table's embrace,
Lies a treasure, a gem, in a quiet space,
Thulium, a mystery waiting to be known,
A chemical element, with a story of its own.

With an atomic number sixty-nine,
It shines with brilliance, yet so benign,
A rare earth metal, so rare and true,
Thulium, oh Thulium, we marvel at you.

Within your nucleus, protons dance,
Neutrons in harmony, taking a chance,
Electrons whirling in orbits bright,
Creating a spectacle, a captivating sight.

Your properties, unique and profound,
Magnetism, conductivity, you astound,
A silvery-gray hue, lustrous and pure,
A symbol of potential, that will endure.

    From medical imaging to lasers so bright,
Thulium, you bring science to new heights,
Your presence in fiber optics, a marvel to see,
Connecting the world, with incredible connectivity.
    Oh Thulium, you hold secrets untold,
A catalyst of progress, a catalyst bold,
As we unravel the wonders you possess,
We're captivated by your brilliance, no less.
    So let us celebrate this element rare,
With reverence and awe, we declare,
Thulium, a testament to nature's grand design,
An element that will forever shine.

TWO

MAGNIFICENT CREATION

In the realm of elements, an enigma resides,
Thulium, a treasure, where science coincides,
With atomic number sixty-nine, it stands,
A luminary among the periodic bands.

A symphony of electrons, dancing in delight,
In valence shells, they shimmer, their energy ignites,
Their orbits a spectacle, a cosmic ballet,
Thulium, the conductor, orchestrating their play.

A rare earth metal, so precious and rare,
In laboratories, scientists tenderly care,
Exploring its mysteries, unlocking its might,
Unveiling the secrets, hidden from sight.

A radiant glow, a whisper in the dark,
Thulium's allure leaves an indelible mark,

Its silvery sheen, captivating to behold,
A testament to nature's alchemical gold.

From lasers to x-rays, its applications vast,
Thulium, a catalyst, in technologies amassed,
A beacon of progress, a bridge to the new,
With every discovery, its significance grew.

Oh Thulium, element of wonder and grace,
In the tapestry of elements, you hold a special place,
Your presence, a reminder of nature's grand design,
A symbol of innovation, that forever will shine.

So let us delve deeper, explore your domain,
Thulium, an element, unique and arcane,
In your atomic embrace, we find inspiration,
To unravel the universe's magnificent creation.

THREE

SYMBOL OF GRACE

Thulium, a hidden gem of the periodic table,
A tale of wonders, I am compelled to fable.
Atomic number sixty-nine, you hold,
A story of rarity, yet to be fully told.

Within your core, a dance of particles so grand,
Protons and neutrons, a delicate band.
Electrons twirl, in their orbits they glide,
A cosmic symphony, where mysteries reside.

Thulium, a treasure with a silvery gleam,
An element unique, like a distant dream.
Magnetism courses through your veins,
Unveiling secrets, breaking boundless chains.

In laboratories, scientists strive,
To unlock your potential, to help us thrive.
From medical marvels to energy's might,
Thulium, you guide us towards the light.

Your luminescence whispers tales untold,
Illuminating pathways with brilliance and bold.
Fiber optics harness your radiant glow,
Connecting the world, wherever we go.

Oh Thulium, a muse for curious minds,
In your presence, innovation unwinds.
A catalyst for progress, a beacon of hope,
Through your essence, human potential can elope.

So let us celebrate your atomic embrace,
Thulium, a marvel, a symbol of grace.
A testament to nature's creative flair,
In you, we find inspiration beyond compare.

FOUR

BOUNDLESS LOVE

Thulium, a jewel in the periodic sea,
A tapestry of nature's chemistry.
Atomic number sixty-nine, you shine so bright,
With your mysteries hidden from sight.

In the depths of science, you quietly dwell,
A rare earth metal, a tale to tell.
Your electrons dance in quantum delight,
Creating a symphony, both day and night.

Thulium, a conductor of magnetic flow,
Guiding the forces that ebb and grow.
Your magnetic properties, a wonder to explore,
Unlocking doors to knowledge like never before.

From lasers to imaging, you pave the way,
In medical realms, you hold sway.
Diagnostic tools, precise and clear,
Thulium, your applications we revere.

Your atomic structure, so elegantly arranged,
A testament to nature's mysteries exchanged.
A silvery luster, a shimmering hue,
Thulium, in awe, we marvel at you.

Oh Thulium, element of allure,
In our quest for understanding, you endure.
A symbol of curiosity and scientific might,
You illuminate the path towards infinite light.

So let us celebrate your atomic embrace,
Thulium, an element of elegance and grace.
From laboratories to the stars above,
Your presence reminds us of nature's boundless love.

FIVE

PRESENCE ECHOES

Thulium, a luminary in the realm of elements,
A celestial dancer with secrets yet to be spent.
Atomic number sixty-nine, you stand tall,
In the periodic table's cosmic hall.

In your nucleus, a symphony of protons and neutrons,
Creating a harmonious balance, a cosmic tune.
Electrons whirl, in orbits they gracefully glide,
Unveiling the wonders of Thulium's pride.

Thulium, a beacon of colors, a kaleidoscope,
A mesmerizing blend of blues and purple hope.
Your radiance, a celestial spectacle to behold,
A shimmering essence, a story yet untold.

In laboratories, scientists delve deep,
Exploring your properties, a treasure to reap.

From lasers to high-temperature superconductors,
Thulium, you inspire us as knowledge disruptors.
 Magnetic allure courses through your veins,
Harnessing the power, breaking free from chains.
Magnets and data storage, your legacy is vast,
Thulium, a guiding light in technological contrast.
 Oh Thulium, an enigma of the periodic domain,
Your brilliance, a testament to nature's arcane.
A symbol of innovation and scientific dreams,
In you, we find a universe of endless streams.
 So let us celebrate your atomic grace,
Thulium, a luminary in the elemental space.
From laboratories to the farthest frontiers,
Your presence echoes, sparking humanity's cheers.

SIX

GLIMPSE THE UNKNOWN

Thulium, a jewel among the elements,
A rare treasure, its brilliance represents.
In the depths of the periodic chart,
Your presence ignites a scientific spark.

A faint whisper in the atomic symphony,
Thulium, your mysteries enthrall me.
Soft and silvery, with a touch of grace,
You weave stories in your atomic embrace.

With magnetic allure, you captivate,
Drawing us closer, we anticipate.
From fiber optics to high-powered lasers,
Thulium, you're the catalyst of scientific blazers.

In the realm of medicine, you shine bright,
Helping diagnose, with accuracy and light.

Your isotopes, a gift for therapy,
Healing lives, with remarkable efficacy.
    Oh Thulium, element of endless possibilities,
Your discoveries unfold with boundless velocities.
A symbol of progress, innovation, and might,
You guide us towards a future so bright.
    So let us celebrate your atomic reign,
Thulium, an element we cannot explain.
Through your essence, we glimpse the unknown,
A testament to the wonders yet to be shown.

SEVEN

THULIUM DIVINE

Thulium, oh element of rarest kind,
In the realm of science, you truly shine.
With atomic number sixty-nine you reside,
A captivating essence that cannot hide.

Silvery-gray, your lustrous face is seen,
A beacon of potential, a vision so keen.
From laboratories to the world outside,
Thulium, you lead us on a wondrous ride.

Magnetic properties course through your veins,
Unveiling mysteries, breaking scientific chains.
In fiber optics, your light travels far,
Connecting hearts, no matter where they are.

Oh Thulium, catalyst of exploration,
Your presence ignites scientific fascination.
From medical imaging to energy's quest,
You pave the way for innovation's best.

So let us honor you, Thulium divine,
In the grand tapestry of elements, you truly shine.
A symbol of progress, discovery, and more,
Thulium, we celebrate your atomic lore.

EIGHT

SHINING IN THE DARK

Thulium, a jewel in the realm of the elements,
A rarity of beauty, its significance never faints.
With an atomic embrace, it captures our gaze,
Unveiling secrets, in its intricate ways.

In the world of lasers, it takes center stage,
Harnessing light, like a poet on a page.
Its luminescence dances with ethereal grace,
Guiding us forward, in this cosmic chase.

Oh Thulium, conductor of scientific symphony,
Your presence conducts innovation's harmony.
From magnetic resonance to high-tech alloys,
You inspire the seekers, the curious, and the wise.

So let us celebrate your atomic might,
Thulium, a beacon in the scientific night.

In laboratories and minds, you leave your mark,
A testament to nature's wonders, shining in the dark.

NINE

LIMITLESS WORLD

In the realm of elements, you hold your place,
Thulium, a treasure with an atomic embrace.
With magnetic allure and a silver sheen,
You captivate our minds, like a radiant dream.

Oh Thulium, element of rare distinction,
Your presence evokes wonder and fascination.
From lasers to nuclear medicine's realm,
You unlock mysteries, guiding science's helm.

A catalyst for progress, you pave the way,
Innovation follows where you may stray.
Through your luminescence, pathways unfold,
Revealing secrets that were once untold.

So let us celebrate your atomic art,
Thulium, the embodiment of scientific heart.
In laboratories, your secrets unfurl,
A testament to exploration, a limitless world.

TEN

HUMAN CURIOSITY

Thulium, oh element of rare allure,
In your atomic embrace, mysteries endure.
A symbol of ingenuity, science's muse,
With each discovery, our knowledge accrues.

In the realm of lasers, your light finds its way,
Guiding us forward, illuminating the way.
With precision and brilliance, you mark the path,
Advancing technology, unleashing its wrath.

Oh Thulium, catalyst of endless innovation,
Your presence sparks scientific elation.
From medical imaging to atomic clocks,
You revolutionize the way knowledge unlocks.

So let us celebrate your atomic reign,
Thulium, an element that will forever sustain.
In laboratories and minds, your legacy thrives,
A testament to human curiosity that strives.

ELEVEN

TO THULIUM

In the realm of elements, you hold your ground,
Thulium, a treasure waiting to be found.
Oh Thulium, with your magnetic allure,
You captivate minds, that's for sure.
A conductor of energy, a luminary of light,
You guide us through the depths of scientific sight.
So let us celebrate your atomic grace,
Thulium, a marvel in this cosmic space.
From lasers to fiber optics, your impact profound,
Unleashing a world where possibilities abound.
In laboratories, your secrets unfurled,
A testament to the wonders of the scientific world.
Thulium, you inspire us to reach higher,
To explore the mysteries of the universe's fire.
So let us raise our glasses and sing,
To Thulium, the element that makes our hearts ring.

A symbol of progress and human quest,
Forever in awe, we hold you to our chest.

TWELVE

SURREAL

Thulium, a name that echoes with grace,
An element that holds a mysterious space.
In the realm of elements, you stand apart,
With your atomic number, etched in every heart.

Oh Thulium, with your radiant glow,
You captivate us, and we come to know
The wonders you bring to the scientific sphere,
Unveiling new frontiers, year after year.

From lasers to medical breakthroughs profound,
You leave an indelible mark, all around.
In high-tech industries, you find your place,
Advancing technology at a rapid pace.

So we celebrate you, Thulium divine,
A symbol of progress and human design.
With every discovery, you ignite our zeal,
Unleashing the power of knowledge, so surreal.

THIRTEEN

LIFELONG DREAM

Thulium, oh element of rare enchantment,
In the realm of science, you invoke wonderment.
With atomic grace, you dance in the void,
Unveiling secrets that were long-avoided.

In laboratories, your mysteries unfurl,
A catalyst for innovation, a precious pearl.
From fiber optics to cutting-edge research,
You inspire minds, reaching beyond the church.

Oh Thulium, conductor of technological symphony,
Your presence orchestrates progress with harmony.
In medical imaging, you paint vibrant hues,
Guiding healers to diagnose and cure the blues.

So let us celebrate your atomic might,
Thulium, shining star in the scientific night.
As we unravel the universe's grand scheme,
You remind us that knowledge is a lifelong dream.

FOURTEEN

INSPIRE

Thulium, element of rare and radiant gleam,
In the periodic table, you reign supreme.
With atomic number sixty-nine, you reside,
A symbol of wonder, where secrets hide.

Oh Thulium, your magnetic allure,
Captivates scientists, seeking to explore.
From lasers to portable X-ray machines,
You unlock possibilities, breaking new routines.

In the realm of technology, you pave the way,
Advancing innovation day by day.
In fiber optics and high-speed communication,
You facilitate connections, bridging every nation.

So let us celebrate your atomic grace,
Thulium, a marvel in this vast cosmic space.
In laboratories and minds, your legacy thrives,
A testament to human curiosity that strives.

As we delve into the mysteries you hold,
The world unfolds, stories yet untold.
Thulium, you inspire, ignite the flame,
Guiding humanity towards progress and acclaim.

FIFTEEN

SCIENTIFIC ANTHEM

Oh Thulium, element of rare allure,
In your atomic heart, wonders endure.
A beacon of science, you brightly shine,
With mysteries and potentials so divine.

In the realms of lasers, your light is pure,
Guiding precision with a steady allure.
From fiber optics to cutting-edge tech,
You empower progress, a future to beck.

Radiant Thulium, in medical quest,
Your isotopes aid, bringing healing zest.
Through imaging, diagnosis precise,
You unlock secrets, a physician's device.

In laboratories, minds explore your might,
Unveiling knowledge, like stars in the night.
Thulium, you inspire, curiosity blooms,
Unraveling secrets, dispelling glooms.

So let us honor you, Thulium, dear,
A marvel of science, shining crystal clear.
In the tapestry of elements, you're a gem,
Forever cherished, a scientific anthem.

SIXTEEN

DISCOVERY'S QUEST

Thulium, element of rare allure,
Your presence in the periodic table, pure.
A symphony of electrons, dancing in grace,
Unveiling mysteries in every trace.

With your atomic number sixty-nine,
You captivate minds, like a celestial sign.
In labs, scientists unravel your powers,
Exploring your essence, for countless hours.

In the realm of magnets, you hold sway,
Aiding in data storage, day by day.
Your luminescence, a beacon so bright,
Guiding the way, through science's light.

Oh Thulium, catalyst of innovation,
You inspire minds, sparking fascination.
In medical realms, you find your worth,
Enhancing diagnostics, bringing healing's birth.

So let us celebrate your atomic might,
Thulium, shining star in the scientific night.
A symbol of progress and discovery's quest,
Forever in awe, we hold you to our chest.

SEVENTEEN

SHIMMER AND GLEAM

In the realm of elements, you shimmer and gleam,
Thulium, the essence of a scientific dream.
With atomic prowess, you captivate the eye,
Unveiling mysteries as the curious pry.

Oh Thulium, conductor of technological might,
You spark innovation with your radiant light.
From lasers to fiber optics, you pave the way,
Empowering progress in every scientific play.

In medical marvels, you find your place,
As MRI scans reveal the body's grace.
Aiding diagnosis, your presence profound,
Guiding healers to the answers they've found.

So let us celebrate your atomic grace,
Thulium, the element that leaves a trace.

In laboratories and minds, your legacy thrives,
A testament to human ingenuity that strives.
    Oh Thulium, with your atomic allure,
You inspire us to embrace discovery and endure.
In the grand symphony of science and art,
You play a melody that resonates in every heart.

EIGHTEEN

ATOMIC EMBRACE

Thulium, rare and precious, a jewel of the periodic table,
Your atomic essence, a scientific fable.
In laboratories, minds unravel your mysteries,
Unleashing potential, pushing boundaries with ease.
From fiber optics to green lasers, you lead the way,
Igniting innovation, casting a brilliant ray.
Oh Thulium, conductor of technological symphony,
Your presence orchestrates progress with harmony.
In medical imaging, you reveal the unseen,
Guiding healers to diagnose, to intervene.
So let us celebrate your atomic might,
Thulium, shining star in the scientific night.
A symbol of curiosity, exploration, and might,
You inspire minds to reach for infinite height.
In the tapestry of elements, you hold a unique role,

A catalyst for change, stirring the human soul.
Thulium, we honor your atomic embrace,
Forever grateful for the wonders you grace.

NINETEEN

POWER SHINES

Thulium, element of rare and radiant hue,
In the realm of science, your wonders accrue.
With atomic grace, you dance in the core,
Unveiling secrets, forever craving more.

From the depths of laboratories, you emerge,
A beacon of knowledge, a boundless surge.
In lasers and imaging, your power shines,
Unveiling the mysteries that the universe confines.

Oh Thulium, conductor of scientific symphony,
Your presence ignites the spark of discovery.
Through the hands of researchers, you unveil,
The hidden truths that the cosmos entails.

So let us raise our voices, let our praise be heard,
For Thulium, the element that leaves us stirred.
In the grand tapestry of elements, you're a gem,
Forever cherished, a scientific anthem.

TWENTY

LASERS TO ALLOYS

In the realm of elements, you hold your place,
Thulium, a mystery, a celestial grace.
With atomic number sixty-nine, you shine,
A symbol of science, discovery's sign.

Oh Thulium, rare earth, lustrous and bright,
You captivate minds with your atomic might.
From lasers to alloys, your applications vast,
Advancing technologies, unsurpassed.

In laboratories, your secrets unfold,
Unveiling new wonders, stories yet untold.
Thulium, catalyst of innovation's fire,
With each experiment, you take us higher.

So let us celebrate your atomic reign,
Thulium, the element that will forever sustain.
In the world of science, you leave your mark,
A testament to human curiosity's spark.

TWENTY-ONE

THE BEST

Thulium, a jewel of atomic grace,
With a radiance that lights up space.
In the periodic realm, you hold your sway,
A marvel of nature's brilliant display.

Your atomic essence, so rare and refined,
Unleashing wonders, expanding the mind.
In the realm of lasers, you find your might,
Harnessing light, painting spectra bright.

Oh Thulium, conductor of scientific dreams,
Guiding us to explore limitless streams.
In the realm of magnets, you hold the key,
Pulsing with energy, setting knowledge free.

So let us embrace your atomic might,
Thulium, shining star, pure and bright.
A symbol of discovery, innovation's crest,
In our quest for understanding, you're the best.

TWENTY-TWO

ADVANCING TECHNOLOGY

Thulium, element of rare beauty and grace,
In the periodic table, you find your rightful place.
With atomic number sixty-nine, you stand tall,
Captivating our minds, captivating us all.

Your magnetic properties, a marvel to behold,
Attracting attention, a story yet untold.
In the world of lasers, you shine so bright,
Unleashing photons, a mesmerizing sight.

Oh Thulium, you light up the scientific stage,
Advancing technology with each passing age.
In medical imaging, you lend a helping hand,
Guiding doctors, helping them understand.

So let us celebrate your atomic allure,
Thulium, a treasure we forever adore.

In the vast universe of elements and more,
You are a symbol of knowledge to explore.

TWENTY-THREE

OH THULIUM, CONDUCTOR

Thulium, element of rare worth,
A gem hidden within the Earth's dearth.
In the periodic table, you proudly reside,
A symbol of ingenuity and scientific stride.

With atomic number sixty-nine,
You captivate minds, like a celestial sign.
In the realm of lasers, you cast your spell,
Harnessing light, a phenomenon to tell.

Oh Thulium, conductor of technological symphony,
Your presence orchestrates progress with harmony.
In medical imaging, you paint vibrant hues,
Guiding healers to diagnose and cure the blues.

So let us celebrate your atomic might,
Thulium, shining star in the scientific night.

As we unravel the universe's grand scheme,
You remind us that knowledge is a lifelong dream.

TWENTY-FOUR

WITHIN THE DEEP

Thulium, oh element of grace,
Within your atomic embrace,
A world of wonders we explore,
With each secret you help us restore.

In laboratories, minds ignite,
Curiosity taking flight,
Unveiling mysteries deep and wide,
With you as our scientific guide.

Oh Thulium, you hold the key,
To realms of possibility,
In lasers, you shine so bright,
Illuminating the darkest night.

Your presence, a catalyst of change,
Innovations you help arrange,
Advancing technology's frontier,
With every discovery we hold dear.

So let us celebrate your atomic might,
Thulium, a beacon of scientific light,
Forever inspiring us to seek,
The knowledge that lies within the deep.

TWENTY-FIVE

INTRICATE DESIGN

In the realm of elements, you stand tall,
Thulium, a wonder captivating all.
With atomic number sixty-nine you reside,
Unveiling mysteries as you gracefully glide.

Your magnetic allure, a captivating force,
Guiding scientists on a cosmic course.
In lasers, you gleam with radiant might,
Painting the world with a vibrant light.

Oh Thulium, catalyst of innovation's reign,
You spark creativity in every domain.
From medical miracles to quantum realms,
Your presence illuminates science's helms.

So let us marvel at your atomic charm,
Thulium, a jewel in the scientific farm.
In the periodic table's intricate design,
You leave an indelible mark for all time.

TWENTY-SIX

ELEMENTAL CHASE

Thulium, element of rare and noble birth,
In the realm of atoms, you hold your worth.
With atomic number sixty-nine you reside,
A symbol of knowledge and scientific stride.

Your electrons dance in energy's embrace,
Creating a spectrum of colors in space.
From deep red to blue, a dazzling array,
Thulium's hues in the scientific ballet.

In lasers you find your purpose and might,
Harnessing photons with precision and light.
From communication to surgery's aid,
Thulium's radiance paves the way.

Oh Thulium, your presence inspires,
In laboratories, scientific desires.
Exploring the mysteries of the cosmos above,
Unveiling the secrets, igniting our love.

So let us celebrate your atomic grace,
Thulium, a marvel in the elemental chase.
A testament to human curiosity's quest,
Forever in awe, we hold you abreast.

TWENTY-SEVEN

PHENOMENON TO BEHOLD

Thulium, oh element of rare delight,
With atomic number sixty-nine, shining bright.
In the periodic table, you stand with grace,
A symbol of knowledge, a captivating embrace.

Your name derived from Thule, a land of myth,
Where legends whisper tales of the ethereal myth.
In laboratories, you reveal hidden truths,
Unveiling mysteries with your atomic pursuits.

From lasers to medical diagnostics, you play a part,
Harnessing energy, igniting the scientific heart.
Your magnetic properties, a phenomenon to behold,
In data storage and quantum realms, stories unfold.

Oh Thulium, conductor of scientific symphony,
Your presence sparks curiosity and epiphany.

In the realm of elements, you hold a unique place,
A catalyst for discovery, a testament to human race.
  So let us celebrate your atomic might,
Thulium, guiding us towards wisdom's light.
In the quest for knowledge, you lead the way,
Forever inspiring minds to explore and sway.

TWENTY-EIGHT

SILENT HERO

Thulium, oh element of rare allure,
A gem among the periodic table pure.
With atomic number sixty-nine you're known,
A world of wonders within your molecular throne.

In nature, you remain a treasure concealed,
But in laboratories, your secrets are revealed.
Your magnetic properties, a scientific delight,
Unleashing potential, pushing boundaries in sight.

Oh Thulium, luminescent in your own right,
You emit a radiant glow, a captivating light.
In lasers, your brilliance finds its stage,
Guiding innovation, turning the page.

So let us celebrate your atomic grace,
Thulium, a marvel in the elemental chase.
From medicine to industry, you play a part,
A silent hero, igniting progress with your heart.

TWENTY-NINE

PURE AND LIGHT

Thulium, element of rare allure,
In the realm of atoms, you endure.
With atomic number sixty-nine,
A treasure of the periodic line.

Your name derived from Thule's ancient land,
A symbol of exploration, ever grand.
In labs and research, you find your place,
Unraveling mysteries, leaving a trace.

Oh Thulium, conductor of scientific dreams,
You illuminate the path with radiant beams.
In lasers, your power finds its voice,
Advancing technology, offering choice.

So let us bask in your atomic glow,
Thulium, a marvel we've come to know.
In the world of elements, you shine so bright,
A beacon of discovery, pure and light.

THIRTY

RADIANT VOICE

Thulium, rare and sublime,
A treasure in the periodic rhyme.
With atomic number sixty-nine,
You grace the table as a gem so fine.

In the realm of elements, you stand apart,
A symbol of science, a work of art.
Your electrons dance in delicate array,
Weaving tales of wonder, day by day.

Oh Thulium, your magnetic charm,
Draws us in with an alluring arm.
In lasers, you find your radiant voice,
Harnessing light, making hearts rejoice.

From medical marvels to technological might,
You guide us towards a future so bright.
Unlocking secrets, expanding our view,
Thulium, we owe so much to you.

So let us celebrate your atomic reign,
A catalyst for progress, breaking every chain.
In the grand symphony of the universe's plan,
Thulium, you shine as a beacon for all of man.

THIRTY-ONE

DANCE OF PHOTONS

Thulium, oh element of wonder and might,
With your atomic number sixty-nine shining bright.
In the depths of the periodic table you reside,
A symbol of knowledge and progress personified.

Your magnetic properties, a scientific fascination,
Harnessing energy with precision and dedication.
In lasers, you create a mesmerizing spectacle,
A dance of photons, a symphony so impeccable.

Oh Thulium, catalyst of innovation and growth,
Your presence inspires minds, igniting creative oath.
In medical advancements, you lend a helping hand,
Guiding surgeons with clarity, improving lives firsthand.

So let us marvel at your atomic allure,
Thulium, a treasure that we gratefully secure.

In the grand tapestry of elements divine,
You shine as a beacon of discovery's sign.
    From laboratories to industries, you lead the way,
Unveiling mysteries, unraveling secrets each day.
Thulium, we celebrate your atomic grace,
Forever grateful for your role in the scientific chase.

THIRTY-TWO

DAY BY DAY

Thulium, oh element of wonder and might,
In the realm of science, you shine so bright.
With atomic number sixty-nine, you reside,
A symbol of progress, a journey to guide.

In medical realms, your presence is sought,
As an aid to heal, a cure to be brought.
Radiating energy, it's your healing touch,
Guiding us towards wellness, oh so much.

In lasers, you find your purpose and place,
Harnessing light with elegance and grace.
From cutting-edge technology to scientific quests,
Thulium, you outshine all the rest.

A conductor of progress, you pave the way,
Expanding horizons, day by day.
Oh Thulium, element of limitless might,
You inspire us to explore, to reach new height.

So let us celebrate your atomic embrace,
Thulium, the marvel of the chemical space.
In the symphony of elements, you play a unique role,
Forever cherished, an eternal soul.

THIRTY-THREE

ADMIRATION

In the realm of elements, a gem so rare,
Thulium, you dazzle with an exquisite flair.
With atomic number sixty-nine,
You captivate our hearts, an enchanting sign.
  Oh Thulium, your energy knows no bounds,
A catalyst for progress, where innovation resounds.
In the realm of lasers, you reign supreme,
Illuminating possibilities, like a vivid dream.
  From medical wonders to scientific frontiers,
You navigate the depths, conquering fears.
Thulium, you unlock secrets with precision,
Advancing knowledge, shaping our vision.
  So let us celebrate your atomic grace,
A symbol of ingenuity, in this cosmic chase.
Thulium, you inspire minds to explore,
Guiding humanity to discoveries galore.

In laboratories and research halls,
You whisper the tales of scientific thralls.
Oh Thulium, element of endless fascination,
We honor your brilliance, with admiration.

THIRTY-FOUR

INFINITE WORTH

Thulium, jewel of the periodic table's realm,
With atomic grace, you overwhelm.
A rare element, in the depths you reside,
Igniting wonder with every stride.

In laboratories, your secrets unfold,
Revealing stories yet untold.
Oh Thulium, conductor of scientific symphony,
You mesmerize with your atomic harmony.

Your luminescent glow, a cosmic dance,
Leading us through the realms of chance.
In lasers, your power finds its voice,
A beacon of innovation, a reason to rejoice.

So let us celebrate your atomic might,
Thulium, guiding us towards wisdom's light.
In the quest for knowledge, you take the lead,
A catalyst for progress, planting the seed.

Oh Thulium, element of infinite worth,
We treasure you upon this Earth.
In the grand tapestry of the universe's plan,
You shine as a testament to the ingenuity of man.

ABOUT THE AUTHOR

Walter the Educator is one of the pseudonyms for Walter Anderson. Formally educated in Chemistry, Business, and Education, he is an educator, an author, a diverse entrepreneur, and he is the son of a disabled war veteran. "Walter the Educator" shares his time between educating and creating. He holds interests and owns several creative projects that entertain, enlighten, enhance, and educate, hoping to inspire and motivate you.

Follow, find new works, and stay up to date
with Walter the Educator™
at WaltertheEducator.com

www.ingramcontent.com/pod-product-compliance
Lightning Source LLC
LaVergne TN
LVHW020134080526
838201LV00119B/3805